GOATs IN SPORTS

TENNIS GOATs

KENNY ABDO

Fly!
An Imprint of Abdo Zoom
abdobooks.com

abdobooks.com

Published by Abdo Zoom, a division of ABDO, P.O. Box 398166, Minneapolis, Minnesota 55343. Copyright © 2025 by Abdo Consulting Group, Inc. International copyrights reserved in all countries. No part of this book may be reproduced in any form without written permission from the publisher. Fly!™ is a trademark and logo of Abdo Zoom.

Printed in the United States of America, North Mankato, Minnesota.
052024
092024

Photo Credits: Getty Images, Icon Sportswire, Shutterstock
Production Contributors: Kenny Abdo, Jennie Forsberg, Grace Hansen
Design Contributors: Candice Keimig, Neil Klinepier

Library of Congress Control Number: 2023948523

Publisher's Cataloging-in-Publication Data

Names: Abdo, Kenny, author.
Title: Tennis GOATs / by Kenny Abdo
Description: Minneapolis, Minnesota : Abdo Zoom, 2025 | Series: GOATs in sports | Includes online resources and index.
Identifiers: ISBN 9781098285685 (lib. bdg.) | ISBN 9781098286385 (ebook) | ISBN 9781098286736 (Read-to-me eBook)
Subjects: LCSH: Tennis--Juvenile literature. | Tennis players--Juvenile literature. | Tennis--Records--Juvenile literature. | Professional athletes--Juvenile literature.
Classification: DDC 796.342--dc23

TABLE OF CONTENTS

Tennis GOATs................... 4

The Greats 8

Scoreboard..................... 20

Glossary 22

Online Resources 23

Index 24

Be it on grass or clay, anyone who goes up against these tennis GOATs will surely meet their match!

From Margaret Court to Novak Djokovic, these tennis players make it a point to set the standard for greatness.

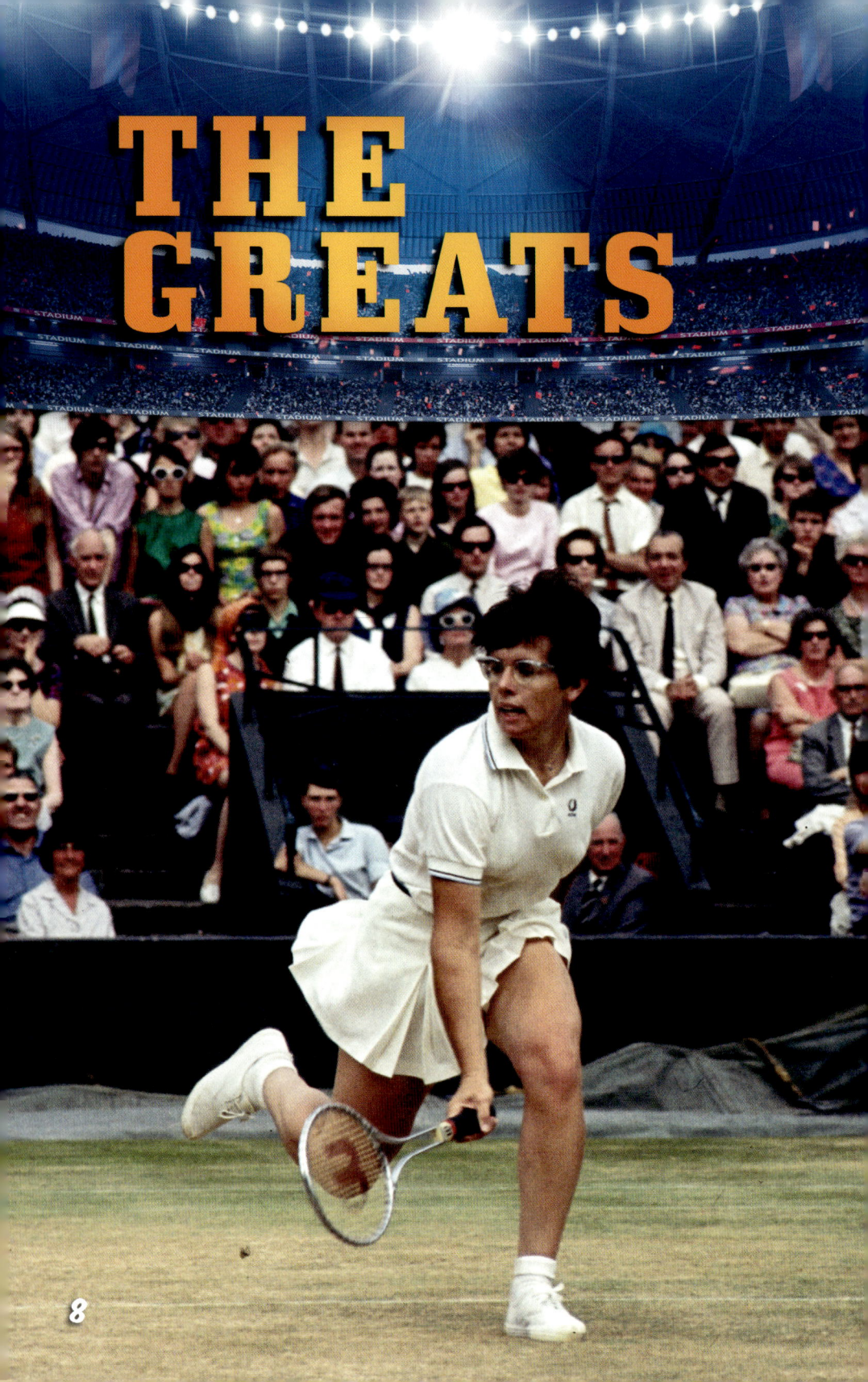

Billie Jean King won her first **Wimbledon** title in 1961. She went on to win it six more times. King also supported **gender equality** in the sport. She was inducted into three different **Hall of Fames**!

From 1960 to 1975, Margaret Court caught the world's attention with her skills on the court. When she finally retired in 1977, Court had racked up a record 64 **Grand Slam** championships. That is the most in tennis history!

Bjorn Borg was such a star in the 1970s, that his popularity was called "Borgmania." Borg won his first **major** in 1974 at 18 years old. By the time he retired at just 26, his 11 major titles were an Open Era record.

Between 1975 to 1986, Chris Evert was ranked either #1 or # 2 in the world. She won 18 **major** singles titles. And her record of 1,309-146 gave her a winning percentage better than any man or woman to step on a professional court.

In 1988, Steffi Graf became the first and only player to achieve the **Golden Slam**. She was also a 22-time **major** champion! She retired in 1999 with 118 titles.

Pete Sampras became the youngest US Open men's singles winner in 1990. He finished his career with 14 **major** championship wins. Sampras was welcomed into the International Tennis **Hall of Fame** in 2007.

Serena Williams has won more **Grand Slam** singles titles than any other player. Williams also brought home four **Olympic** gold medals! She retired in 2022 as an inspiration to future players.

Roger Federer ruled the court with his amazing skills. In 2018, he became the first player to claim 20 **Grand Slam** men's singles titles. Federer also earned a record eight **Wimbledon** titles!

Rafael Nadal went pro in 2001. At 15 years and 330 days old, he became the youngest tennis player to win a professional match. By 2024, Nadal had won 20 **Grand Slam** titles and two **Olympic** gold medals!

Novak Djokovic is a tennis GOAT for many reasons. He is the only player ever to complete a **Career Golden Masters**. Djokovic also holds the record for **Grand Slam** singles titles with 24!

SCOREBOARD

Tennis continues to be watched by people around the world. Fans witness these court greats serve up history with each match.

GLOSSARY

Career Golden Masters – when a player wins all nine Masters 1000 events at least once each.

gender equality – a situation in which access to rights or opportunities is unaffected by gender.

Golden Grand Slam – when a player wins all four Grand Slam tournaments and the Olympic gold medal during their career.

Grand Slam – when a player wins all four major championships in the same calendar year.

Hall of Fame – the group of highly celebrated people honored for their achievements in a sport or other activity. In tennis, it is called the International Tennis Hall of Fame.

majors – in tennis, one of the four most important tournaments. They include the Australian Open, the French Open, Wimbledon, and the US Open.

Olympic – of or relating to the Olympic Games. The Games are the biggest international athletic events held as separate winter and summer competitions.

Wimbledon – the oldest and most respected tennis tournament in the world.

ONLINE RESOURCES

To learn more about the GOATs in Tennis, please visit **abdobooklinks.com** or scan this QR code. These links are routinely monitored and updated to provide the most current information available.

INDEX

Borg, Bjorn 11

Court, Margaret 6, 10

Djokovic, Novak 6, 19

Evert, Chris 12

Federer, Roger 16

Graf, Steffi 13

King, Billie Jean 9

Nadal, Rafael 17

Olympics 15, 17

Sampras, Pete 14

Williams, Serena 15